THIS BOOK BELONGS TO:

_____

WELCOME TO KENTUCKY

Dedicated to all the explorers.

ISBN 978-1-958985-70-0

www.joeysavestheday.com

A Mimi Book

The name "Kentucky" comes from the Iroquoian word "Ken-tah-ten," meaning "land of tomorrow."

KENTUCKY

Kentucky was the 15th state to join the union.
It officially became a state on June 1, 1792.

Kentucky shares land borders with seven states: Illinois, Indiana, Ohio, West Virginia, Virginia, Tennessee, and Missouri.

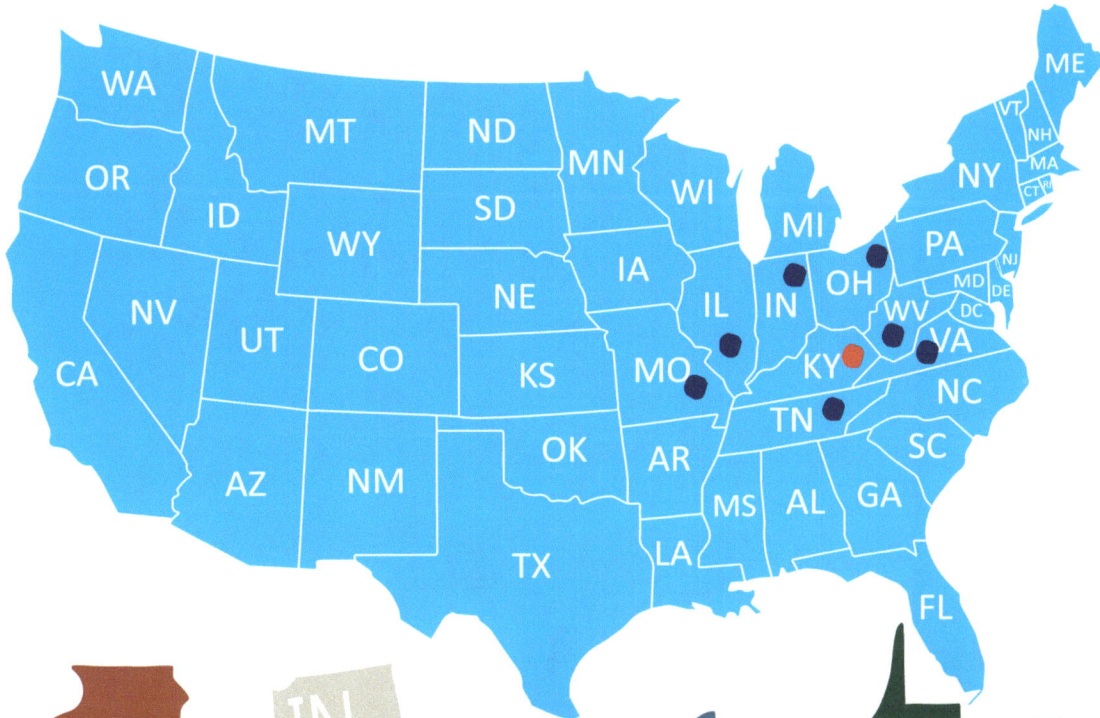

ILLINOIS

INDIANA

OHIO

WEST VIRGINIA

VIRGINIA

TENNESSEE

MISSOURI

7

Frankfort is the capital of Kentucky. It officially became the capital in 1792.

Frankfort, Kentucky, has an estimated population of 28,600 people.

Kentucky is the 37th largest state in the United States.

Kentucky

Louisville, Kentucky

There are about 4,588,370 people who live in the state of Kentucky.

Lexington, Kentucky

11

CREATIVITY

The origin of Post-it Notes is Cynthiana, Kentucky! This is where 3M initially produced the sticky squares that would later illuminate desks and inspire creativity across the globe.

KENTUCKY

Abraham Lincoln was born on February 12, 1809, in a tiny log cabin on Sinking Spring Farm in what was then Hardin County, Kentucky. Today, that place is part of LaRue County.

There are 120 counties in Kentucky.

Kentucky

Here is a list of 20 of them:

Adair	Carlisle	Henry	Owsley
Ballard	Elliot	Johnson	Russell
Bath	Floyd	Lincoln	Spencer
Boone	Grant	McCreary	Whitley
Caldwell	Greenup	Monroe	Wolfe

Cumberland Falls in Kentucky is known for its enchanting moonbow, an ethereal rainbow created by moonlight! On clear nights during a full moon, the mist from the waterfall contributes to this breathtaking spectacle.

Kentucky

Kentucky's state tree is the Tulip Poplar.

Kentucky boasts more navigable waterways than any other U.S. state, with the exception of Alaska.

K

Covington, Kentucky

Colonel Harland Sanders founded Kentucky Fried Chicken (KFC) in Corbin, Kentucky.

Fried Chicken

The northern cardinal, a vibrant and captivating bird, serves as the official state bird of Kentucky, a title it has held since February 26, 1926.

Kentucky proudly named the Viceroy butterfly its official state butterfly in 1990. Often mistaken for the Monarch, the Viceroy stands out with its elegant orange wings and a bold black line across the hindwings

Viceroy butterfly

Monarch butterfly

The official state flower of Kentucky is the Giant Goldenrod (Solidago gigantea), a striking perennial plant known for its vibrant yellow blooms.

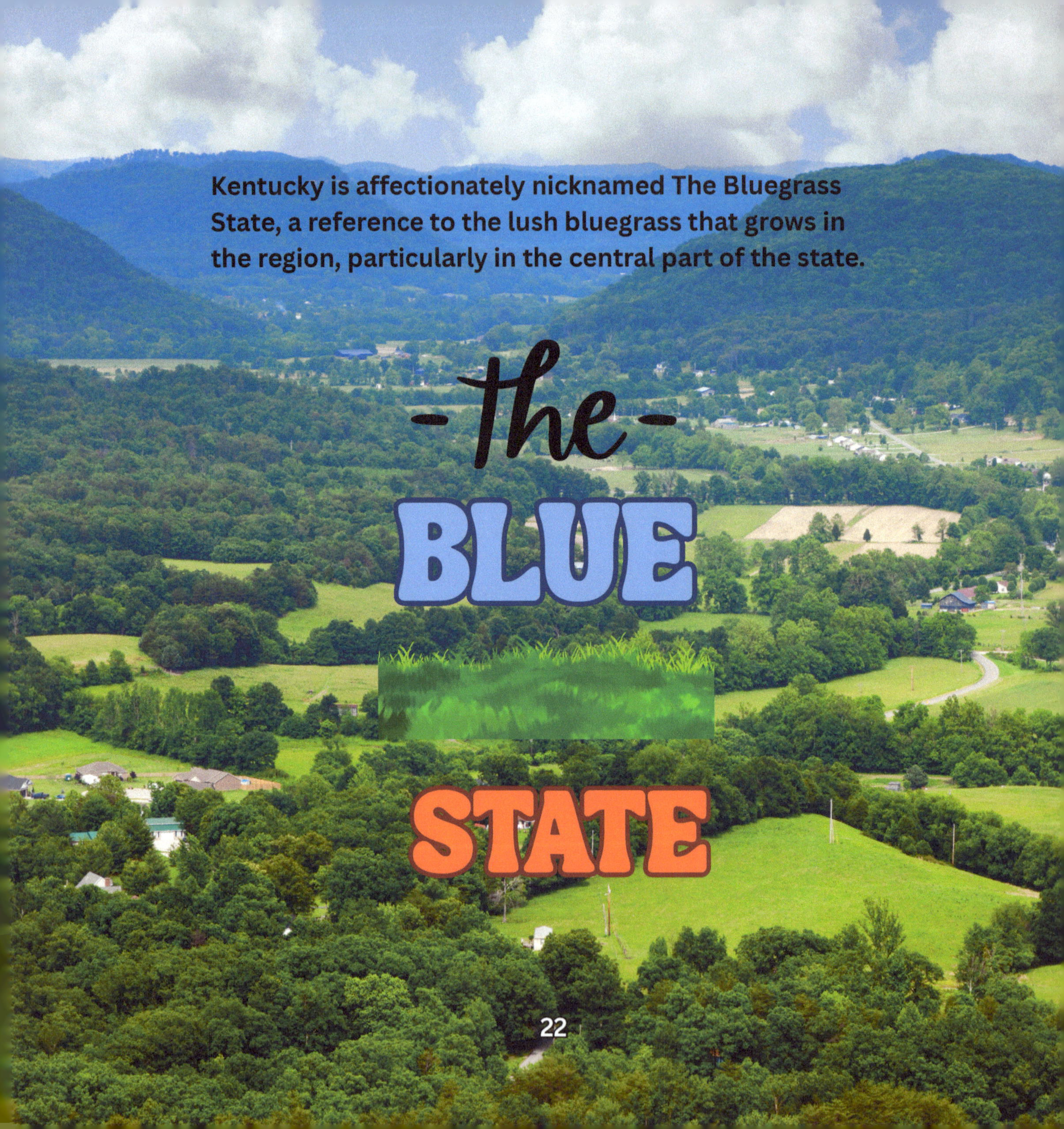

Kentucky is affectionately nicknamed The Bluegrass State, a reference to the lush bluegrass that grows in the region, particularly in the central part of the state.

-the-

BLUE

STATE

In 1769, Daniel Boone climbed a tall hill in Kentucky called Pilot Knob. When he looked out, he saw miles of wild land and forests. He decided to explore! Later, he helped make a trail called the Wilderness Road so families could travel west and start new lives. That trail helped Kentucky grow!

Daniel Boone National Forest

KENTUCKY
KENTUCKY
KENTUCKY
KENTUCKY

The abbreviation for Kentucky is KY.

KY

On March 26, 1918, Kentucky officially adopted its state flag. The design was created to celebrate the state's rich history and the important values that make Kentucky special.

Some of the crops grown in Kentucky are corn, oats, soybeans, and wheat.

Some of the animals that live in Kentucky include bats, bears, coyotes, deer, raccoons, and river otters.

Kentucky experiences significant temperature fluctuations throughout the year. The state recorded its highest temperature of 114 degrees Fahrenheit in Greensburg on July 28, 1930. In contrast, the lowest temperature documented was -37 degrees Fahrenheit in Shelbyville on January 19, 1994.

Hot

Cold

Abraham Lincoln, the 16th president of the United States, was born on February 12, 1809, in a small log cabin in Hodgenville, located in LaRue County.

The state motto, "United we stand, divided we fall," reflects the values of unity and resilience among its residents. This motto was officially adopted in December 1792.

UNITED
we stand

Kentucky

The University of Kentucky Wildcats baseball team competes in NCAA Division I and is part of the Southeastern Conference (SEC), known for its fierce competition and athletic excellence. With a strong tradition of academic achievement and standout players, the Wildcats are a proud symbol of Kentucky's sports legacy.

Kentucky's football team is called the Wildcats, and they play at Kroger Field in Lexington. Their colors are blue and white, and their mascot is a wildcat named Scratch! The team has been playing since 1881 and competes in the Southeastern Conference (SEC), one of the toughest college football leagues.

BATTLE

During the Civil War, Kentucky saw many battles as both Union and Confederate soldiers fought for control. One of the biggest was the Battle of Perryville in 1862, where thousands of troops clashed in the hills.

KENTUCKY

WAR ZONE

Every spring, the Kentucky Derby gallops into action at Churchill Downs in Louisville, Kentucky. It's the most famous horse race in America and has been held every year since 1875!

Can you name these?

I hope you enjoyed
learning about
Kentucky.

To explore fun facts about the other 49 states,
visit my website at www.joeysavestheday.com.
You'll also find a wide variety of homeschool
resources to support joyful learning at home.
If you enjoyed this book, I would be grateful if
you left a review. Your feedback truly helps.
Thank you for your support!

TIME
TO SAY
GOODBYE

Check out these other interesting books in the 50 States Fact Books Series!

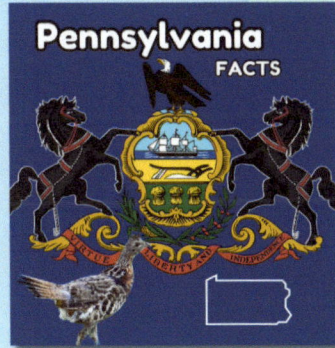

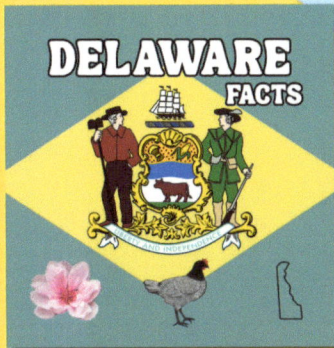

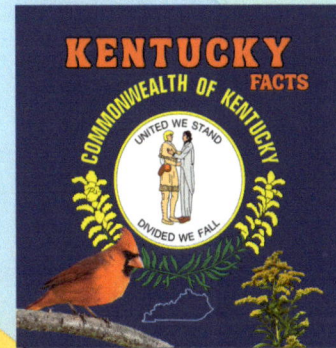

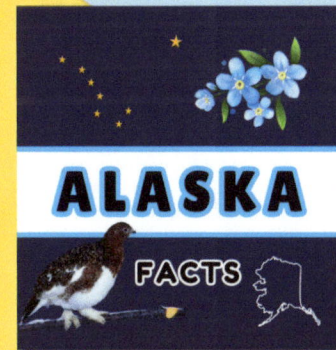

OHIO FACTS

Pennsylvania FACTS

TEXAS FACTS

DELAWARE Facts

CALIFORNIA REPUBLIC

CALIFORNIA FACTS

KENTUCKY FACTS
COMMONWEALTH OF KENTUCKY
UNITED WE STAND
DIVIDED WE FALL

CONSTITUTION
WISDOM JUSTICE MODERATION
IN GOD WE TRUST
GEORGIA FACTS

ALABAMA Facts

ALASKA FACTS

www.mimibooks.com

www.ingramcontent.com/pod-product-compliance
Lightning Source LLC
Chambersburg PA
CBHW041549040426
42447CB00002B/106